Mind Maps® *for kids*

Study Skills

Tony Buzan

with Jo Godfrey Wood

D1340101

thorsons

Mind Map® is a registered trademark of The Buzan Organization.

Thorsons
An Imprint of HarperCollins*Publishers*
1 London Bridge Street,
London SE1 9GF

The website address is:
www.thorsonselement.com

and *Thorsons* are trademarks of
HarperCollins*Publishers* Limited

First published by Thorsons 2004

13

© Tony Buzan, 2004

Tony Buzan asserts the moral right to
be identified as the author of this work

A catalogue record of this book
is available from the British Library

ISBN-13 978-0-00-717702-8

Cartoons and Mind Map® illustrations by Stephanie Strickland

Printed and bound in China by
RR Donnelley APS

Dedication

This book is dedicated to all the kids out there who dream of getting straight As, know they can, but haven't got the right formula to unlock their amazing minds and limitless creativity. This book contains that formula and will help you make all those dreams come true.

Acknowledgements

Many thanks to all the 'Master Mind Mapper' kids who have helped me with this book: Edmund Trevelyan-Johnson and Alexander Keene who used Mind Maps to help them get into the schools of their dreams; the pupils of Beechwood School in Slough who proved through Mind Maps what geniuses they all are; the children of Berryhill School in Scotland for their outstanding Mind Maps; the children of Willow Run School in Detroit; the children in Singapore's Learning and Thinking Schools; the children of Seabrook Primary School in Australia; and all the other 'Mind Map' kids all over the world that I've been fortunate enough to meet!

With special thanks to my wonderful Mind Maps for Kids Support Team at Thorsons: Carole Tonkinson, Editorial Director; Susanna Abbott, Commissioning Editor; Natasha Tait, Book Designer; Sonia Dobie, Cover Art Design Manager; Nicole Linhardt, Senior Production Controller; Liz Dawson, Publicity Manager; Laura Scaramella, Foreign Rights Director; and Belinda Budge, Managing Director.

A big thank you also to Jo Godfrey Wood, Writer, and Stephanie Strickland, Illustrator, who together have helped bring this book alive with their superb writing and illustrations; to Jenny Aviss, Principal of Wetherby Schools for encouraging everybody to Mind Map; to Helen Evans for editorial advice; and to Caroline Shott, my incredible Literary Manager whose energy and dedication constantly amaze me. Finally, a special thank you to my Mind Maps for Kids Home Team: Lesley Bias for her 'flying fingers'; Vanda North for introducing kids around the world to the magic of Mind Maps; my brother, Professor Barry Buzan, for his decades-long support of me and the Mind Mapping concept; and to my mum, Jean Buzan, who has always encouraged this 'grown-up' Mind Map Kid!

Contents

Letter from Tony   *vi*

Chapter One – Rev up for Revision!   2
    Revision? Say What?   4
    I Know I Know This   5
    Let Your Brain Take the Strain   6
    The Five-times Repetition Formula 7
    Make Friends with Your Right Brain 10
    Right Brain, Right Revision   11
    Fixed Up for Revision!   15
    Hot Subject for a Mind Map   19

Chapter Two – Getting into the Mind Mapping Groove   22
    Seven Steps to Exam Success   26
    Tooled Up and Clued Up   28
    Check Out the Mind Map Checkmap   29
    Get Drawn into Revision   32
    Mind Map to Success   33

Chapter Three – Get Sorted!   34
    All Systems Go   37
    Mind Map Motivation   38
    Read Around!   43
    Chilling   44
    Get Out and Move About   45
    A Little Treat for Every Feat!   46
    How Much Time?   46
    Get to Know Yourself!   46
    Build Up Your Confidence   48

Chapter Four – Mind Maps in Action   50
    Make Mind Maps Work for YOU!   53

Mind Mapping English   **56**

The Empty House   *58*

Mind Mapping Maths   **62**

Recognizing Shapes   *62*

Collecting Data   *64*

Mind Mapping Science   **68**

Life Cycles   *68*

Reversible and Irreversible Changes   *69*

Mind Mapping History   **74**

Elizabeth I and the Armada   *74*

The Egyptians and Tutankhamun   *78*

Mind Mapping Geography   **82**

Volcanoes   *82*

Mind Mapping Languages   **86**

Pick a Colour   *86*

Mind Map Shopping List   *87*

Mind Mapping Citizenship   **90**

Reuse it, Don't Lose it!   *94*

Chapter Five – Don't Let it Get to You!   **96**

Don't Bottle it Up   **99**

Doodle Down-Time   **99**

De-Stressing Techniques for Mental Athletes   **100**

Chapter Six – Exam Attack   **106**

Chic Technique   **109**

Read Before You Write   *109*

Master it With Mind Maps   *111*

Write it Right   *111*

Read to Lead   *112*

Rest and Be Ready   *112*

Chapter Seven – What a Breeze!   **114**

Party Time!   *116*

Resources   *120*

Index   *121*

Letter from

Did you think there were only the three Rs (**Reading**, '**Riting**, '**Rithmetic**)? Well, they've added a fourth – it's called **Revision**!

Do your parents nag you about revision and exams (as well as your mobile bill and tidying your room)? Teachers do it, too, and they can really do your head in – I know it.

I used to get really stressed out about exams. I knew I HAD to do them but I was scared because my memory seemed to seize up when it had to hold lots of **facts**. I didn't like taking notes and what's more, I didn't like re-reading my notes even if I'd taken any (often, I'd already forgotten what they meant!). On top of that, I thought I'd drown in the number of different topics I had to **revise**.

All in all, I hated doing revision, exams and the idea that people would think I was a 'failure' if I didn't do well in them. Then I asked myself a few questions (try asking yourself these questions, too).

How many hours had I spent learning:

★ *maths and numbers*
★ *language and literature*
★ *science, geography and history?*

THOUSANDS!

BUT ...

 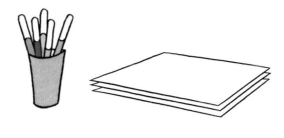

How many hours had I spent learning about:

* *memory*
* *note-taking*
* *my creative powers*
* *my brain power*
* *what happens to my memory after learning something*
* *revision techniques*
* *exam techniques?*

NONE!

So I began to study our fabulous brains and discovered that they love **colour**, **excitement**, **variety**, **energy**, **movement** – all the things black and white lines of revision notes DON'T offer. The more our brains can get **INTERESTED** in something, the easier it is to get them whirring in anticipation and *in* the information goes and *in* it stays. **RESULT**!

If you're like me and dream up all sorts of excuses NOT to revise, then let me share my **invention**, the Mind Map, which will make revision a thousand times more interesting and infinitely easier. *Anyone* can use it and all you'll need are: paper, felt-tip pens and your **BRAIN**! You will then work *smarter*, not *harder*. When you're working smarter you can take more breaks, forget about stress, have lots more **fun** with your friends, AND get far better exam grades.

So, what are we waiting for? Let's get started!

Rev up for Revision!

Mind Maps **will make your revision a** breeze **– they'll**

help you get sorted, organize **your work,** stroll **through**

exams and get excellent **results!**

Hi! Have you, by any chance, got exams coming up in the not-too-distant future? Has your home become a battle zone? Do your parents constantly nag you about doing **revision**? Got round to doing any yet? Yes? No? Maybe? Hang on a minute! Just who are you kidding? Get real!

Like Hell-ooo-oo! You may be fooling everyone else that you have been doing some revision, but YOU know that you haven't. Started panicking yet? Has revision become the 'R-Word', spoiling your entire life? Well, it's time to wise up and get up for it! **Up for revision**! YIKES!

Revision? Say What?

There's no getting out of it. So what does that ominous word 'revision' mean anyway? Well – it really means to '**see again**', to have another look at something, to 're-view' it, so that your brain can **re-learn it**, **re-think it** and **memorize** it.

Forget about revising being a hard slog; a painful sweat over a pile of boring books. Let your brain **PLAY**! Let it have **FUN**! It will then **remember** things more easily. When you finally hit the exam room, you will find that you can answer exam questions without any problems and **pass** with **flying colours**!

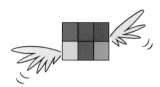

Think about **daydreaming**. We all do it. In fact, you may be on for an A* in Daydreaming Studies. But, contrary to what teachers may tell you, day-dreaming is not just gazing into space and it's not a waste of time. It's actually an **awesome brain activity**. When you are revising using **Mind Maps** to help you, your brain daydreams about everything you have learnt and plays around with it. This helps to fix it in your mind.

Mind Maps not only help your brain revise your work, they will help you **cruise** through exams! Hard to believe? Can it possibly be that easy? **It's true**! You can do it too!

This book will show you how to remember everything you need to know, get sorted, use your brain and even enjoy revising and exams. By the time you've finished reading it, you'll actually be looking forward to revision! Yes you can, really! On top of that – you'll be looking forward to getting those grades you know you deserve! RESULT!

I Know I Know This!

Do you sometimes have problems **remembering** things, like the name of an actor in a film or who sang that hit you liked last summer? It's on the tip of your tongue – you DO know it really, but you just can't bring it to the front of your mind. We all suffer from this. What usually happens is that if you get your brain to think about something else for a few minutes, you'll suddenly remember the thing you were trying to remember in the first place. This is OK (though very annoying) in daily life, but it's a NIGHTMARE if it happens in an exam, isn't it?

Let Your Brain Take the Strain

Here are a few questions (they're NOT exam questions) …

Q Does your memory resemble a sieve and does it seize up when you try to cram lots of things into it at once?

Q Do you have a hard time concentrating? When you look at a blank exam paper (or one of those nasty-looking printed ones) does your brain seem to grind to a halt?

Q Do your notes look boring and make your brain switch off?

Q Do you get a mega-mental block at the very mention of the word 'revision'?

Q Do you put off revision until the last moment and then do it in a mad panic? Do you HATE revision and DREAD exams?

Q Do you get bad exam nerves? And do you DREAD getting your results because you know you could have done better?

Don't worry if you answered 'yes' to any, or all, of these questions. All you need to do is to harness the awesome power of your brain, and exams will be **EASY**.

One of the most important things you can do when you are revising is to max up your **MEMORY**. In an exam you need to be able to remember everything you need INSTANTLY because you are working against the clock. How can you make your **memory** work **instantly**? Well, first of all we'll look at how your memory works.

How long does something you have learnt stick in your **brain**? A few hours, a day, a week, two weeks? Well, the sad truth is that after a very short time – less than a day after the lesson – you forget most of what you learnt. UNLESS you do something to stop this forgetting process.

> '*Without effective revision you forget 80% of new stuff you've learned in a day. Scary or what?!*'

What can you do? You can **REVIEW** what you've learnt, and use Mind Maps. Reviewing means 'having another look': **REVISING**! If you review your work **FIVE** times altogether, your memory will be able to keep the information in your brain **FOREVER**!!!!!! So don't just sling your notebooks into the bottom of your bag. When you get home, take a few minutes to check out what you wrote. It will save you loads of revision time when it comes to exams later on.

The Five-times Repetition Formula

Here's the secret to reviewing information five times to make it stick. The first time should be an hour or so after you've first read or learnt something, for example, when you get home. The second the day after (so take another look the next day after school). The third should be about a week later, the fourth one month later and the fifth and final time six months later. Then it's yours, FOREVER! And how can you remember what you need to review and when? You've got it! By drawing a Mind Map!

Left Alone Means Right is Left!

Did you know that your brain is divided into **two halves**, each of which has a different way of working? You use the **left side** of your brain for **thinking** about things like **words**, **numbers** and **lists**. You use the **right side** of your brain when you are using your **imagination**, when you are daydreaming, when you are seeing colours, and when you are involved in rhythmical activity. So when you are dancing to your favourite tunes, your right side is in action. Which side do you think you mainly use when you are doing normal school work and revising? Yes! The **left side**, of course.

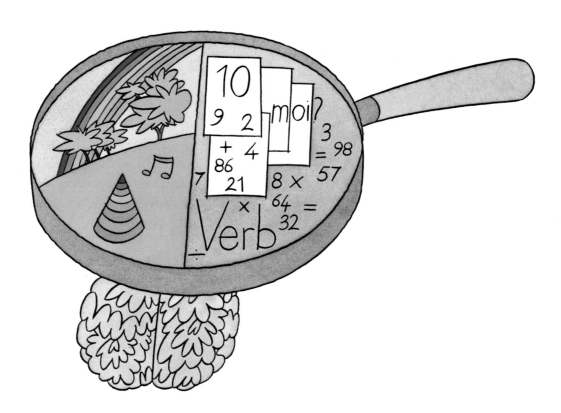

'Two halves make a whole'

Think about this **astounding fact**. When you are doing **schoolwork** and revising in the normal way you are really only using half of your brain – the left half. The right half is going to waste! That's a big shame, because you could be making **use** of the right half, too, to **excel** at your work, to help you do your revision and to help you **ace exams**! How? By letting your wonderful brain get to work on **colour** and **pictures** as well as the normal lines and word lists.

Make Friends with Your Right Brain

Try this little **experiment**! (You don't need to be in a science lab to do it!)

Think of one of your **friends** (it could be your best mate). What pops into your brain? Is it a word? Is it a list? Or is it a mental image (a 'brain picture') of that **person**? I bet it was the **image**! So the easiest way to remember your friend would be to draw a picture of him or her, wouldn't it? Because your brain automatically wants to use its **visual**, **colourful**, **pictorial** side.

'A picture is worth a thousand words'

Right Brain, Right Revision

You can use this **pictorial** (right) side of your brain when you are doing **revision**. How? By drawing pictures and using colours. Your brain will find it **MUCH** easier to remember **pictures** and **colours** and will therefore be able to remember the **FACTS** and **IDEAS** that go with them. How? By using Mind Maps! But what exactly is a Mind Map?

A Mind Map is a special kind of brain-friendly diagram that helps you to think, imagine, remember things, and plan and sort information – in short, it's a perfect tool to help you do your revision.

If it sounds complicated, it's not. Mind Maps are easy to do and all you need are some coloured pens, a blank sheet of paper and … your brain! Start now by drawing a **Mind Map** of all your mates and the things they like doing most. Take a look at the Mind Map of Mel's friends on pages 12–13 to give you an idea of the kind of things you could include.

★ *Get a blank piece of paper and turn it on its side (to 'landscape' format).*
★ *Put a picture or symbol of yourself in the centre.*
★ *Then draw a line coming out from the centre for each of your friends. Put the name of that person on top of the line.*
★ *Next draw a picture of that person on each line, but at the end.*
★ *Now draw little lines coming off the big lines – one for each of the things they like doing.*
★ *Draw a little picture for each thing they're interested in.*

If the thought enters your head that you can't draw, banish it – you **CAN**! Everybody can draw and that includes **you**! Mind Maps will release the artist in you.

Now you have all your **mates** on one sheet of paper! What could you use it for? You could use it for remembering everyone's **birthday**. No excuses for forgetting to send a card! And if you want to get them a present, your Mind Map shows you what they're **interested** in.

climbing

October 10

RICHARD

football

computers

rollerblading

November 20

MELINA

reading

My

My Friends Mind Map

nds

AIMEE

July 6

judo

hip-hop

computer

games

CAT

singing

May 3

shopping

WILL

movies

March 14

gym

cycling

Once you have got the hang of it, tell all your friends so that they can get into the Mind Mapping **groove**, too.

Fixed Up for Revision!

Some would say that revision is boring, however you do it!

Well, it can be. But it need not be. Think about it. Most revision is boring because we do it in a way that is boring for our **amazing**, **creative** and **powerful brains**! We get bored by **reading** lists and lines of black words on white pages, with no exciting pictures or colours to tempt the imagination or excite the eye. We switch off and our minds start wandering about aimlessly, waiting for something more stimulating to come along. This is when we actually stop being able to revise and remember things. What our **brains** really crave is **colour** and **excitement**! This is where Mind Maps can really help our brains focus and concentrate and make an enormous difference to our ability to remember things, too.

But HOW?

Because Mind Maps use **colour** and **pictures**, they help us to use both sides of our brains and make it easier for us to think, plan, organize, remember and take control. Let's put this idea to the test.

What do you mean, my spelling isn't much good? That's my algebra!

15

Read this piece of text about the Fire of London:

THE FIRE OF LONDON

'On September 2nd 1666 a fire started in the City of London in the King's baker's house in Pudding Lane.

The fire spread rapidly, though to begin with the poorer people stayed in their houses until the very last minute.

Lots of people ran towards the River Thames and threw their possessions into it.

Attempts were made to stop the progress of the fire by pulling down houses in its path, but finally parties of sailors blew up houses with gunpowder, to make wide gaps that the flames could not reach across. The Fire burned down eighty-four churches, including old St Paul's, many fine buildings and hundreds of wooden houses, which were built very close together. It destroyed filthy alleys and narrow streets and cleansed the town of all traces of the Plague.'

By Will Penfold
Disaster Reporter
© *Daily News*

Without checking back at what you've just read, try to answer these questions:

QUESTIONS

1. When did the fire happen?
2. Where did it start?
3. How did they try to stop it?
4. How many churches were burnt down?
5. Which big church was destroyed by fire?
6. What helped the fire spread?
7. What was the only good thing to result from it?

Answers
1. September 2nd 1666.
2. In the King's bakery in Pudding Lane.
3. By blowing up houses and creating big gaps to prevent fire spreading.
4. Eighty-four.
5. St Paul's.
6. The houses were wooden and built close together.
7. It destroyed the Plague.

Did you get the answers all correct after only one read-through? Probably not. You would have to be very observant to be able to do that, and have a very good memory as well.

If you read it again, and made a big effort to remember all the important bits, how long do you think you would be able to remember them for? Ten minutes? One hour? Two hours? Until tomorrow? Until next week? Indefinitely?

Well, you might remember bits and pieces until the end of today or even until tomorrow, but unless you keep looking at it, it's going to be a struggle. Your brain gets fed up with lines of **black text on lined paper**. Your brain's so lively that it needs something more! It needs colour and pictures on plain paper to help fix those exciting facts in your memory – all the things that normal school textbooks don't always give you. All these things will make you more interested and more able to remember. Give your brain some colours and pictures and it will be able to remember SERIOUS amounts of information. Remember, a picture is worth a thousand words.

Why are football players never asked for dinner?

Because they're always dribbling!

Hot Subject for a Mind Map

How could you sort the **facts** from the piece of text about the Great Fire of London to make them easier to remember?

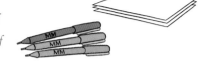

1. *First of all you could grab a small collection of colourful felt-tip pens and an ordinary piece of white paper. Turn the paper on to its side (to 'landscape' format).*

2. *Then you could draw some flames and write 'Fire of London' (your main idea) in the middle in big lettering.*
3. *Now you could choose four things that you can remember to do with the Fire of London and draw branches coming out from the central idea. Use a different colour for each of the four things.*
4. *After that some other smaller ideas might pop into your brain that you could put on smaller branches coming from the bigger ones. Get the idea?*

Before long, you have put down all the **ideas** and things you can remember about the Fire of London on one sheet of paper. Easy or what?

What sort of **ideas** did you put on your first Mind Map? There are many correct choices, so if yours are different from the ones shown here, don't worry. These are just examples of choices. If you look at the **Mind Map** example on the next page you will see that there are lots of little **images** of the different ideas. Again, these help keep your brain interested and help you **remember** the facts better. Now try adding some of these to your Mind Map – if you haven't drawn some on already! Don't worry about how accurate your drawings are. Just make them as **lively** and **colourful** as you can. The main thing is that they should each **REMIND** you of one particular aspect of the Fire of London. Join them on to the branch they illustrate. Let your **imagination** run **wild**!

Now have a good look at your Mind Map and try to remember where each piece of information is on it and what colour your branches are. This will help you when you try to remember all the information later – and is particularly good when you are in an exam: your brain will find it much easier to recall facts that are strongly associated with a particular colour or image.

Rev up for Revision!

19

1666

pudding lane

bakery

STARTED

King's

death

PLAGUE

ended

The Fire of London Mind Map

halls

St. Paul's

B

BUILDINGS

churches

84

HOUSES

wooden

alleyways

blown-up

Getting into the Mind Mapping Groove

Read on to find out **loads** more

about how to make marvellous

Mind Maps.

In this chapter we give you lots more useful **details** about how to make really amazing Mind Maps and use them for revising all sorts of different **subjects** (not just the Fire of London!).

But don't think that Mind Maps are only helpful for revision. You can use them for all sorts of things. For example, when you have finished your **exams** you could do a Mind Map to help you plan a **celebratory** party for all your friends (*see pages 116–19*)!

Without turning back to Chapter 1, how much can you **remember** about the Fire of London now? Plenty! And what helps you remember so much about it? Yes! The **colours** you chose and the **pictures** you drew on your Mind Map helped your brain to **remember** things! Your brain just loves all that cool visual stuff!

Teacher: Lucy, let me hear you say your tables.

Lucy: Dining table, kitchen table, bedside table, coffee table.

Tony's Mind Map Tips

What are Mind Maps for?

Mind Maps help you ...

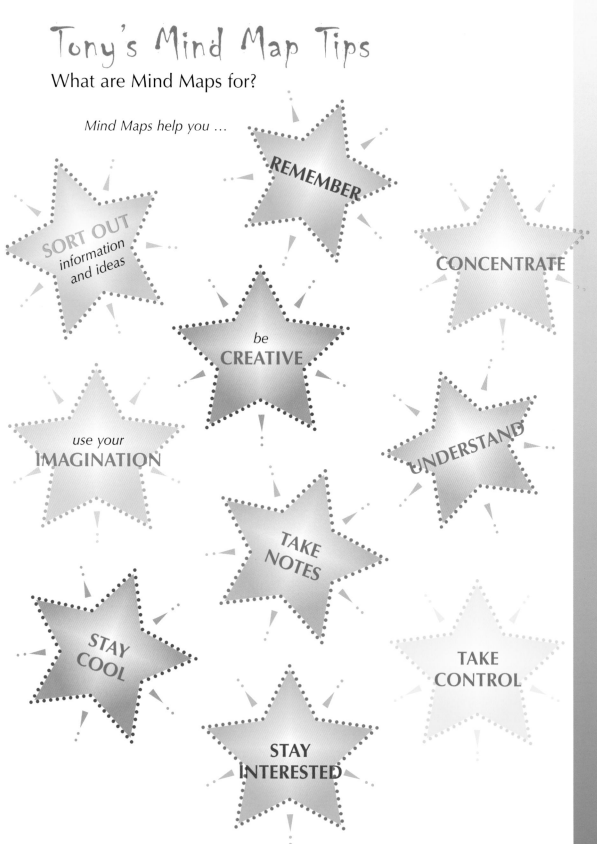

REMEMBER

SORT OUT information and ideas

CONCENTRATE

be CREATIVE

use your IMAGINATION

UNDERSTAND

TAKE NOTES

STAY COOL

TAKE CONTROL

STAY INTERESTED

Seven Steps to Exam Success

Let's take a more detailed look at your Mind Map instructions. They're mega-simple.

1. *Take a sheet of plain white paper. Don't used lined paper – it will stop your ideas flowing. Turn the paper on to its side ('landscape' view). Starting at the centre gives your brain the freedom to spread out in all directions and to express itself more naturally.*

2. *Take some brightly coloured felt-tip pens. Pick out your favourite colours.*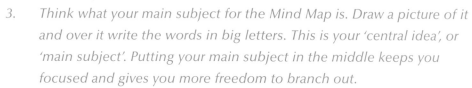

3. *Think what your main subject for the Mind Map is. Draw a picture of it and over it write the words in big letters. This is your 'central idea', or 'main subject'. Putting your main subject in the middle keeps you focused and gives you more freedom to branch out.*

4. *Choose a colour and draw a main branch off the central picture. This is the first idea you have connected to the main subject. Make the branches thicker where they join on and have them tapering off at the ends. Write the idea, using only one word, in capital letters, filling up the length of the branch. Do the same for all the other main ideas you have, but using a different colour for each one.*

5. *Now let your brain think of more ideas for sub-topics. Draw thinner branches coming off the main ones and draw a little picture for each one (on its own line). Put the words in small letters along the branches. Pictures help your brain remember and concentrate, giving you more freedom and flexibility (make sure they are touching the branches, as when they're connected on the page they'll be connected in your brain – you'll understand and remember them better).*

6. *If you have even more ideas to add to your sub-topics, add extra, even smaller, branches, words and images.*

7. *Now you have everything you need to remember about your subject all on one sheet of paper, with pictures and colours to help your brain.*

Tony's Mind Map Tips

This is how to organize a hierarchy of information on your Mind Map, so that it is set down in the right order:

★ Put your *central idea, topic* or *image in the centre.*
★ Put your **main ideas or topics** *on the main branches.*
★ Put your **sub-ideas or topics** *on the secondary branches.*
★ Put your **sub-sub-ideas or topics** *on the little branches.*

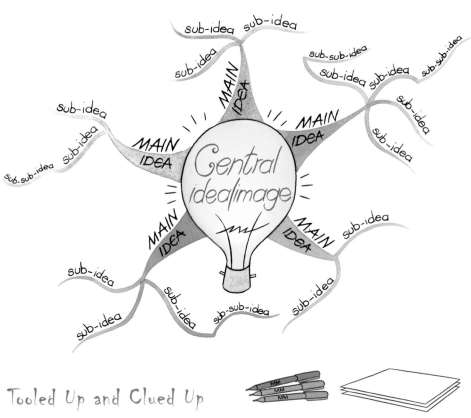

Tooled Up and Clued Up

Mind Map tools are ridiculously simple. Use them anywhere, any time you need to take **notes** or do a bit of revision. Your **tools** are: your **plain white paper**, your **felt-tip pens** and your **brain**!

Put your Mind Maps on your wall. Having them on display will **reassure** you (and your parents) that you are doing **major** amounts of revision. Use as **MUCH COLOUR** and as many **PICTURES** as you possibly can. This will help your brain **REMEMBER** facts.

Check Out the Mind Map Checkmap

To make things even **easier**, here's a special Mind Map **Checkmap**. This is useful when you are using your **IMAGINATION**, like when you are making up a story or **SORTING OUT** information. It works like this. Whenever you are making **notes** or dreaming up a story, use the following questions to plan your **Mind Map**. They are: What? Why? Where? When? Who? Result! (not necessarily in that order).

Now try doing an **original** Mind Map of your own, using the Mind Map **Checkmap**.

For example, say you need to write a short **essay** and you have been given the subject **Your Hobby**. Let's see how Mind Maps can help you **organize** the **information** for you.

1.   *Start off by drawing a colourful picture of your hobby.*
2.   *Then think of your Mind Map Checkmap. Draw a thick branch for the first question, which is What? As you are drawing it and colouring it in, think about your hobby.*
3.   *Then draw the Why? branch.*
4.   *Then draw the Where? branch.*
5.   *Then draw the When? branch.*
6.   *Then draw the Who? branch.*
7.   *Finally draw the Result! branch.*
8.   *Add on any sub-branches to add to the details of your essay and write in all the words (remember, one word at a time).*
9.   *Draw any little pictures to illustrate your Mind Map.*

The Mind Map on the next page is of Matt's hobby, skateboarding. There are no right or wrong answers when it comes to Mind Mapping – every one is **different**.

skateboard helmet

wallet

SKATEBOARD

WHAT?

money

train pass

excitement

HAPPINESS

RESULT!

skills

achievement

tricks

FUN!

WHY?

slips

slides

balance

movement

turns

speed

My Hobby Mind Map

SKATE-PARK
WHERE?

train
ramps
refreshments

WEEKENDS
WHEN?

saturday
morning

sunday
afternoon

FRIENDS
WHO?

Chloe
Chris

Reena
Joe

When you've finished your Mind Map try writing out your whole essay about your hobby, using your Mind Map as a **guide**. Does it make things **easier**? Notice how **What?**, **Why?**, **Where?**, **When?**, **Who?** and **Result!** give you a **structure** upon which to base your essay.

Get Drawn into Revision

Again, don't worry if, like many people, you feel you can't **draw** well. Do you like **doodling**? Most people do(odle)! It's not a waste of time. It's a way of daydreaming with a pen in your hand. It helps you **concentrate**, helps you **imagine** things and boosts your **memory**. And with the help of some colourful felt-tip pens, you can really do some fantastic doodling! Grab a piece of paper and try it out to see what your **daydreaming** right brain comes up with. It will make you feel much better about drawing.

The more colourful and fun your doodles are the more **memorable** they will be! And the more **colourful** your pictures/doodles are, the easier your brain will find it to remember facts and organize your thoughts. A Mind Map is really a mega-doodle! Think of it that way.

Mind Map to Success

So you can see that **Mind Maps** are extremely useful for directing your daydreaming, which will help you **remember facts** and **plan** essays. How is this going to help your revision and help you pass those important exams? Well, first of all, you will be able to **remember** things amazingly easily and second, you will be able to use Mind Maps to plan exam answers astoundingly quickly. No more staring at a blank exam paper nervously waiting for ideas to fall from the sky! We'll tell you all about **using** them during exams in Chapter 6 *(see page 106)*.

Now you've learnt how to do a Mind Map it's time to get organized. See you in Chapter 3!!!!

Why aren't football stadiums built in outer space?

Because there's no atmosphere!

First Reminder

'Five-times repetition equals long-term memory'

Get Sorted!

If you revise **well, you'll** remember **MORE** than you learnt in the first place. How**? Your brain's got an amazing ability to** latch **on to loads of other** connected **things.**

Some people (well OK, a few) are highly organized and always seem to have tidy rooms, but the rest of us tend to be a bit more untidy. However, whichever type of person you are, you need to sort your workspace to do your revision. What kind of work environment do you think YOUR brain prefers? What do you NEED in order to do your revision well?

Tony's Revision Tips

Brain-friendly suggestions for your revision:

★ *A well-lit space (to let your brain's 'eye' see what's going on).*
★ *A desk, table or worktop (you need space to spread out).*
★ *A fairly comfortable chair (yeah, but no dozing off yet!).*
★ *Pens, pencils and felt-tip pens (for making marvellous Mind Maps).*
★ *Books, files and plain paper (for brain stimulation).*
★ *A pinboard for your Mind Maps (everything at a glance – wicked!).*
★ *Important bits and pieces (posters, certificates, mascots).*

Looks like something has exploded in here!

WARNING, WARNING, DISTRACTION ALERT!

Watch your back! There are four monster **temptations** waiting for you, each of which may try to stop you doing your revision. They are **TV (and videos)**, **games consoles**, **computers** and your **mobile phone**. They beckon and tempt you ('Watch me!', 'Play with me!', 'Push my buttons!' 'Speak to me!').

Think of all of these as being **treats** that you can do in between spells of revision. If you use a computer for **research** make sure that you only use it for that during your revision time and NOT for playing games. With all the extra time you save on new-style revision with Mind Maps, you will soon be able to return to them, so chill!

All Systems Go

Your desk is going to become the **launch** pad for your revision, so it is important to get it organized. Get rid of anything you don't actually need and sort all your **notes** and **books** by **subject**. Put them in a row on a shelf nearby. Put all your **felt-tip pens** and **pencils** in a handy container and reserve a little space for bits and pieces that you like to have around you, such as **CDs** and **mascots**. Being organized will unclutter your mind and save you time in the long run.

Get Sorted!

Mind Map Motivation

Now you've got a workspace you can get started on **planning** your revision.

As early as possible in the school year, get a large sheet of paper (you could stick four A4 sheets together) to make your **Revision Mind Map**. The point of this is to remind you to do revision in the first place and then to give yourself a pat on the back for doing it. This Mind Map is going to keep you going and **cheer** you up at the same time. **Motivation!** You will be able to see that you are **achieving** things. And that will make you feel **less stressed**.

Some people get into a terrible state about when to actually start doing revision. They put it off day after day, week after week, until they are propelled into it in a **mad panic** at the very last minute. No need for this!

Revise your work AS YOU GO ALONG!

Don't Let it Fester!

From the start of the school year, every day, when you sit down to do your normal **homework**, make a habit of looking through what you did today in school. If you are unsure about anything, ask your mates or your Mum or Dad to quickly run through it again with you. Don't leave it to fester in your mind.

Five-times Repetition Reminder

Remember: **five-times repetition equals long-term memory**. So if you revise something five times over six months, it will stick in your brain forever *(see page 7)*. When you make a habit of regularly looking over your work as you go through the term, you will find that you are doing your revision all the time. Sounds scary? It won't be, because you will be doing it a **little bit at a time**, and it will have become a **habit**. Even better, when exam time looms, YOU WILL HAVE ALREADY DONE YOUR REVISION!!!

Five-times Repetition = Long-term Memory

 1st Repetition – An hour or so after learning or reading something

 2nd Repetition – A day later

 3rd Repetition – A week later

 4th Repetition – A month later

 5th Repetition – Six months later

One Page Fits All

Another thing that will **really** help you is if you do a Mind Map of all the things you need to learn. Not only will this help you to get a good overview of what you need to do, but it will also help you see what you've done – and all on one page. The revision Mind Map on the next page is an example of the kind of overview Mind Map you might find helpful (see page 42 for tips on drawing your own). What with Mind Maps and repetition you're going to 'A'ce your exams.

What did the Spanish farmer say to his hen?

Olé!

Get Sorted!

populations

settlements

rivers

coasts

localities

environmental

issues

volcanoes

glaciers

GEOGRAPHY

numbers

integers

$\frac{7}{8}$

fractions

percentages

120%

ratios

decimals

MATHS

vocabulary

FRENCH

grammar

composition

CITIZENSHIP

rules

behaviour

democracy

racism

rights

duties

laws

groups

pressure

Revision Overview Mind Map

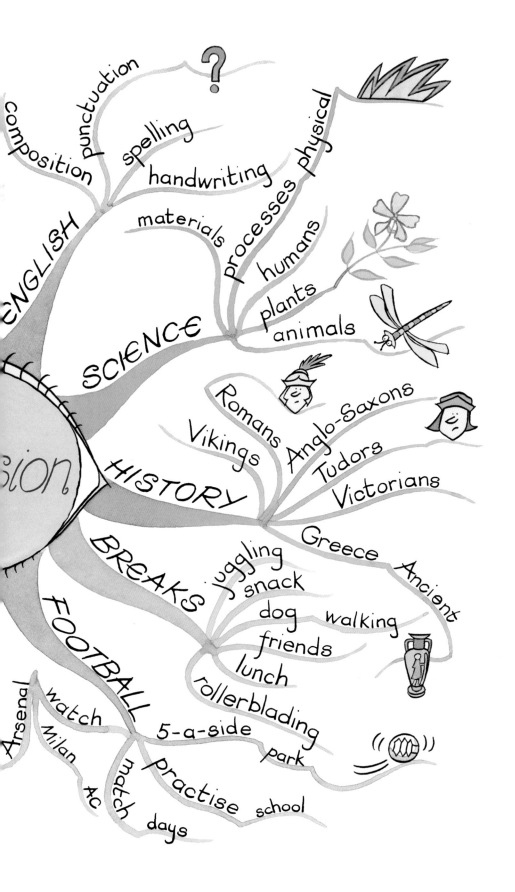

composition
punctuation
?
spelling
handwriting

ENGLISH

materials
processes physical
humans
plants
animals

SCIENCE

sion

Romans
Anglo-Saxons
Vikings
Tudors
Victorians

HISTORY

Greece
Ancient

BREAKS
juggling
snack
dog
walking
friends
lunch
rollerblading
park

FOOTBALL
Arsenal
watch
Milan
AC
match
practise
5-a-side
school
days

Over to V-you!

Now try drawing your own Revision Overview Mind Map with what you need to revise. Get a piece of paper and your coloured pens and:

1. *Draw a picture of something you associate with revision in the middle.*

2. *On the main Mind Map branches, write down all your subjects, one on each branch (choose a bright colour for each).*

3. *On the little branches, put down the main topics of each subject (the ones we've shown are examples – yours may be different). Draw as many little reminder pictures as you can.*

4. *Each time you revise a topic, reward yourself with a tick or a sticker. This will mean that you can see, at a glance, exactly how much revision you have done for each subject and for each topic. Don't be slack and avoid revising your least-favourite subjects. They actually need more time and attention than the others. You will eventually have many more ticks or stickers on your least-favourite subjects, won't you?*

5. *Lastly, stick your Revision Mind Map up on your wall.*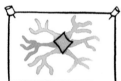

Tony's Revision Tips

★ Start looking back over your work right from the start of the school year, even if you only spend a few **minutes** on this. Make a habit of taking a little time after school looking at what you have done so far – look at everything you did today and everything you have done so far this term.

★ The more **often** you go over your work (up to five times), the more easily it will stick in your **brain**, and it will stick there right up to (and during) the exams.

★ Spend more **time**, more often, revising your **weaker** subjects.

★ Ask others (mates, parents, teachers, brothers, sisters) for **help** if you don't understand something.

★ Five-times repetition equals long-term **memory**.

Read Around!

You may have heard people going on airily about 'reading around the subject' and wondered exactly what they were talking about. Well, all it means is having a look out for other **books** and **sources** of information (not just school textbooks) on a **subject**. You could start looking at useful **websites** and **magazines** as well as **books**. See if there are any relevant **TV** programmes coming up. Go to the local **library** and see what other books on the subject you can find. This will broaden your **knowledge** and help you keep **interested**. You will be able to tap into other people's **viewpoints** and **opinions**, which will all help to make the subject **INTERESTING**. If it is interesting, you are interested – a sure-fire route to **SUCCESS**.

When you are **reading around**, you can use Mind Maps to take **notes**, so that you can **remember** what you have read. Tackle this in the same way as you did for the Fire of London *(see page 20)*. Read the text, put the **main topic** in the centre, put the important things you need to remember on the **main branches**, and **secondary** things on the **little branches**. You now have a one-page record of what you have read on the internet or in the library. Stick it in your **Mind Map file** with your other notes or on your wall with your other Mind Maps.

Chilling

Give yourself a little **break** when you've
actually done what revision you intended to
do and take time to chill. Think of revision
breaks as an essential part of your revision **plan** and add them to your Revision
Mind Map. You could
spend a few minutes
playing with your dog
or chatting to a friend.
But don't be tempted to slide off
and watch TV for an hour or so.
Don't let the break **BECOME** the activity.

But **REMEMBER**. You must return to your
revision after the break time (about 5–10
minutes). Be strict with yourself about
breaks. Become the master or mistress of
your own **destiny**. If it helps, set your
alarm to remind you to **get back** to
it. You need to be in **control** – don't
let other things (such as the 'four
monsters') control you.

Don't be put off if you have friends who boast about how they have done
10 hours' revision without taking a break. They are **dreaming**! For a start they
are only saying it to make you feel bad or to kid themselves because they
are panicking about revision. Plus they are probably **exaggerating** (massively!).
If they have been revising without breaks, they won't have been revising
EFFECTIVELY. The person who takes regular, **short breaks** is the one who
SCORES!

Get Out and Move About

It's **important** to take **PHYSICAL** breaks, too. **Exercise** gets more 'high-octane fuel', or oxygen, into your brain, making you sharper, quicker and more alert. Your brain will become a formula-one racing car instead of a clapped-out old banger. When you have been sitting still revising, you need to move around and free up your body. This will keep you healthy and keep your brain working well, too. If you **play** a regular sport, build the occasional game or match into your revision timetable (put them on your Revision Mind Map as well as your **subjects**). You need to get out and move about. If you play a team sport, you will enjoy meeting up with friends and doing something **DIFFERENT**. Even if you're not a sports freak, take time out to get **moving**. Dance around to your favourite tunes or rollerblade round the block. All work and no play will make your brain VERY dull indeed!

A Little Treat for Every Feat!

Having a treat and **rewarding** yourself for completing what you set out to do is important. It gives you something to look forward to and makes you feel that you've **accomplished** something. Choose something little that really will feel special and worth working towards, but keep it simple, keep it small! We're not talking major rewards yet! (Those are reserved for **AFTER** the exams!)

How Much Time?

When it gets near to exam time (say, at the start of the exam term), you need to think about how much **time** to spend revising each **subject**. You can write approximate times up on your Revision Mind Map. Remember that five-times repetition equals long-term memory. You'll find that each time you go back to a **topic** you'll be more familiar with it, and you will then need to spend less time on it. Give yourself a **tick** (or sticker) on the Mind Map when you have done what you'd planned to do. Your weaker subjects should receive a few more ticks (or stickers) than your stronger ones.

Get to Know Yourself!

What sort of a **person** are you? Ever thought about that before? The kind of person you are affects almost everything you try to do and whether you are **successful** or not. Including revision and **passing exams**. You have **strengths** and weaknesses, just like everyone else on this planet. What you need to do is identify your strengths and weaknesses and then set about **improving** your weaknesses.

For example, say you are good at Geography but not so good at History? What do you need to do? You need to spend a bit **more time** revising your History during the year.

What other kinds of strengths and weaknesses do you have?

Think about what sort of person you are. For example, do you feel more **lively** and **alert** in the mornings or are you a **night-owl** sort of person, who likes working in the evenings? If you are an **early bird**, make use of this and do a bit of revision in the mornings. Later in the day, use the evenings for reading around the subject in a more relaxed way. This way you will be using your personal qualities (the way you already are) to your own **advantage**.

Build up Your Confidence

Confidence is the key to a lot of things in life. If you feel confident about something, you can **enjoy** it and be good at it. Well, the same applies to schoolwork and revision. If you think that you don't like a subject, even hate it, it's probably because you took longer to understand some aspect of it when you were first **taught** it and this has destroyed your **confidence** in it. Maybe you missed some school because of illness, or the teacher didn't explain something very well. You thought to yourself 'Oh no – everyone else **understands** this, but I don't, I must be thick!'

Well, for a start, you probably weren't the only one. But this one little setback has gradually eaten away at the whole subject in your mind – enough to make you feel that you can't enjoy it and do well in it any more. Take heart and don't give up on it! If you do a **Mind Map** of a subject that you like, you will find that there are **connections** with subjects that you think you DON'T like. Because everything is connected to everything else. You will realize that you really **DO** like those subjects after all.

All Subjects are Connected

You may like football and play for your school but hate Maths because you don't think you're any good at it. Well, think again! To be good at football you have to be good at Maths, as you have to calculate all sorts of angles and distances in your mind to get the ball where you want it. So, next time you're set a question on geometry, put your mind on the football field!

Second Reminder

'Five-times repetition equals long-term memory'

If you do have something that you don't **understand**, which is making you HATE that subject, don't be afraid to ask someone to help you. The first obvious person is your teacher. But if you don't feel that you want to ask them, ask a mate, your brother or sister, your parents or a relative. Anyone who you feel you can trust and who will take you seriously.

As your **confidence** builds up, you will soon find that you don't actually **HATE** that subject after all – in fact, you even quite **like** it!

Mind Maps can help your confidence by **showing** you how much you really know about a subject.

Why is six afraid of seven?

Because seven eight nine!

Mind Maps in Action

Mind Maps **will make your English, Maths, Science, History, Geography, Languages and Citizenship revision** a breeze!

Mind Maps can be used in many different ways. Get to know yourself a bit by thinking about how **YOUR brain** works (think about what you **LIKE** doing and what you DON'T LIKE doing) and see how you can use Mind Maps.

How Do You See Mind Maps Working for You?

★ *Does your* MEMORY *need jogging?*

★ *When you read some factual text, do you need help* SORTING OUT *the ideas in it?*

★ *Do you feel your* CONCENTRATION *wandering while you are trying to read and understand something? Mind Maps can help you* FOCUS *and stay focused on what you are doing.*

★ *When you need to* **DREAM UP** *a great idea for a story, does your brain seem slow and sludgy? Mind Maps will set your mind free. You can be more* **CREATIVE** *using Mind Maps.*

★ *Mind Maps will also help you take logical notes for revision, help you* STAY INTERESTED *and become* MORE *interested.*

★ *Mind Maps will help* CALM *you down if you feel a bit jittery.*

★ *Mind Maps will help you* GAIN CONTROL *over your revision.*

Your brain loves Mind Maps! Mind Maps let you use your brain the way it was **designed** to be used, using both left and right sides at once (*look back at page 8*), and using your brain's **natural** brilliance at thinking in **colours** and **pictures**.

A picture is worth a thousand words. So if a Mind Map contains eleven pictures it must be worth eleven thousand words.

Make Mind Maps Work for YOU!

Now let's see how Mind Maps can be used in all sorts of **different** ways for your various subjects.

- ★ *You could use a Mind Map to REMEMBER a plot in a book you are reading – maybe a 'set' book.*
- ★ *You could use a Mind Map to SORT OUT and remember 'themes' in information.*
- ★ *You could use a Mind Map to PLAN a creative writing project or an essay.*
- ★ *You could use a Mind Map to ORDER and remember facts.*
- ★ *You can use a Mind Map to MAKE NOTES when you are revising.*

> If you revise well, you'll remember **MORE** than you learnt in the first place. How? Your brain's grappling hooks latch on to loads of other connected things.

In the **subjects** set out on the next few pages, there are plenty of **suggestions** about how you can use Mind Maps in different ways. They are simply suggestions.

For each of your subjects, it is a good idea to **draw** an **Overview Mind Map**, which includes all the topics you need to revise. Your Revision Overview Mind Map (*see pages 40–1*) will only have **space** for the **main topics**, so you will need a more detailed Mind Map for each subject. This will help you feel that you **KNOW** what you have to cover – and it's all there on one page rather than in a long, boring list or lots of pages. For example, for **Science** you need to draw a Mind Map a bit like the one drawn on pages 54–5.

changes

evaporation

heat

rocks

dissolving

separation

filtration

MATERIALS

S
curr
to

exercise

muscles

diet

HUMANS

joints

circulation

bones

reproduction

teeth

Overview of Science Topics Mind Map

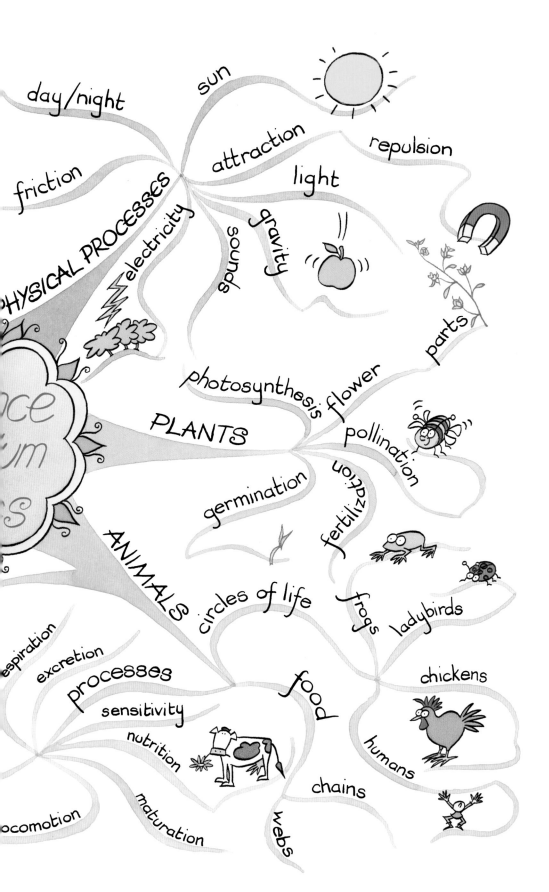

day/night

sun

attraction

repulsion

friction

light

PHYSICAL PROCESSES

electricity

gravity

sounds

parts

photosynthesis flower

PLANTS

pollination

germination

fertilization

ANIMALS

circles of life

frogs

ladybirds

respiration

excretion

processes

chickens

sensitivity

food

nutrition

humans

chains

locomotion

maturation

webs

Mind Mapping English

Say you need to write a story in your **English** exam, but your brain has (temporarily) run out of **good ideas**. The title of the story is The Empty House. Sounds a bit boring doesn't it? Any ideas yet? Let's see if **drawing** a Mind Map can help you. Take out your Mind Map tools (remember? paper, felt-tip pens, brain) and put the **main idea** in the **centre**. Choose some **bright colours** and away you **go**!

★ *In the centre draw the empty house. Colour it and add any little touches you think might be interesting. Remember to use lots of different* colours. *This is a very good way of getting your imagination going.*

★ *Now draw your main branches coming out from the* **centre** *picture.*

★ *Then really free up your* **imagination!** *Think of all the exciting and interesting possibilities that* **could** *be connected to this house. Use the What-Why-Where-When-Who-Result Mind Map Checkmap (see page 29) to give you* **inspiration.** *For example, What is the house like? Where is it? When did the events in the story take place? Who lived there? Why? What happened?*

ooohhh!

★ *Add the* **sub-topic** *information to the main branches, using as many symbols, pictures and colours as you can.*

★ *Carry on using your imagination to dream up* **exciting** *and* **intriguing** *details and add them, too. The more you can add, the more interesting and unusual your story will be.*

★ *Keep on going until you have enough* **information** *on your Mind Map to start writing out your story.*

Tony's Mind Map Tips for English

Mind Maps will help you:

★ *Take **notes** and collect ideas from a variety of sources*
★ *Unlock your **imagination** for creative stories*
★ ***Plan** factual essays*
★ ***Remember** grammar and punctuation*

From Mind Map to A* Exam Essay

When you have finished **brainstorming** the exam question with your **speedy summary Mind Map** – *see page 111* for tips on drawing Mind Maps in exams – you can then use your Mind Map to **structure** your essay. Think of each main branch on your Mind Map as a section and use these sections as the **basic structure** for your essay. Start by looking at each of the main branches and number them in order of **priority** – which would it make more sense to write about first? For example, take a look at The Empty House Mind Map on pages 58–9.

There is no right or wrong answer when it comes to choosing which branch comes first – it'll just make a different essay!

Mind Maps in Action

The Empty House Mind Map

empty

house

exploring

playing

Kim

Dave

CHILDREN

Tom

equipment

dusty

INSIDE

kitchen

props

living-room

stairs

attic

bedrooms

Branches Sussed – Write It Up, No Fuss!

One good way to start this essay would be to begin writing about the 'INSIDE' main branch describing the house, which would set the scene of the **action** and make the house the **focus** of your essay. Alternatively, you could start with the 'CHILDREN' main branch, describing who it was who **discovered** the house. This would engage the reader more with the children and make them the main focus – the house would be one of their experiences. The thing to remember is that there are no right or wrong answers – a **different order** would simply mean a **different essay**!

Once you have decided on the order of your main branches you can start writing. Drawing the Mind Map will have unlocked your imagination so you'll find it easy – your pen will fly across the page!

The sub-branches from the main branches will help you with the **detail** of what you write for each section of your essay. For example, let's say you decide to start with the 'INSIDE' main branch. Its sub-branches explain what the house was like, so you could start the essay by introducing the dusty house with its **eerie** atmosphere, empty rooms and **secretive** spiders. When you've finished writing about that branch you would then move on to the next one you've selected, say the 'CHILDREN' branch, and write about that, and so on until you have written up **all** the branches.

The short story opposite is an example of what you could write from the Empty House Mind Map. It starts with the 'CHILDREN' main branch and follows round the others in a clockwise direction.

Here is one possible version of the story (yours will be different).

One summer's day, many years ago, three children, Kim, Dave and Tom, were wondering what to do with themselves. It was a sizzling hot day. They had already been fishing, swimming in the lake, had climbed the big tree in the field, and had tried to build a treehouse. All of a sudden Kim remembered the derelict house on the other side of the village. It stood in the middle of a large field and had been empty for many years. No one could remember who had lived there and no one seemed to know anything about it.

The three made their way to the house and gingerly opened the front door. It was unlocked and ajar, the dried-out wood creaked and the hinges squeaked. Inside, all was quiet. A thick layer of dust covered everything, but the children could make out an array of rusty kitchen items

on the table. Possessions lay scattered everywhere.

Treading carefully on the broken-down staircase, they made their way upstairs. In the attic, amongst heaps of broken furniture, they spotted a closed trunk. Prising it open, they discovered an array of old velvet jackets, lace-collared shirts, trousers with rosettes on, slouch hats complete with ostrich feathers, and high, soft suede boots. Excitedly they pulled on the clothes and admired the results in a broken old mirror. They looked uncannily like the Three Musketeers. Giggling nervously they started fencing with some old swords they found lying in the corner.

Just then, they noticed the wind billowing a red velvet curtain and footsteps sounding behind it. They froze in their tracks, eyes popping, holding their

breath. A strange, deep voice boomed 'Who goes there?' Hearts in their mouths, Kim, Dave and Tom threw down the swords, and scattering the dressing-up clothes as they tore them off, tumbled down the stairs, out of the door and across the field as fast as their legs could carry them. Speechless with fright, they stumbled back home, mentioning their adventure to no one.

Several days later, they decided to return to the house. They went into the field and looked across at where the house should be. But there was nothing there – not a trace. Thinking they must have walked into the wrong field, they went into the field next door. But there was nothing there either. Asking around in the village, they found that no one had heard of such a house ever having existed.

Mind Maps in Action

61

Mind Mapping Maths

At first glance, you might not think **Mind Maps** can be used for revising Maths. But they **can**! Think of all the various things you need to **learn**.

Recognizing Shapes

Take shapes, for example. You need to remember all the three-dimensional shapes and know what they look like. A Mind Map is **perfect** for this. You have a quick **visual** reference to help you whenever you need it and the **colours** will help fix the names in your brain. For example, in future, when you are trying to remember what a square-based pyramid looks like, your brain will remember that you drew it in blue on your Mind Map. The **act** of drawing the shapes also helps **fix** them in your **memory**.

Tony's Mind Map Tips for Maths

Mind Maps will help you:

★ *Remember* facts *and* formulas
★ **Sort** *and remember data*
★ **Sort** *information*

What did the arithmetic book say to the geometry book?

Boy, do we have our problems?

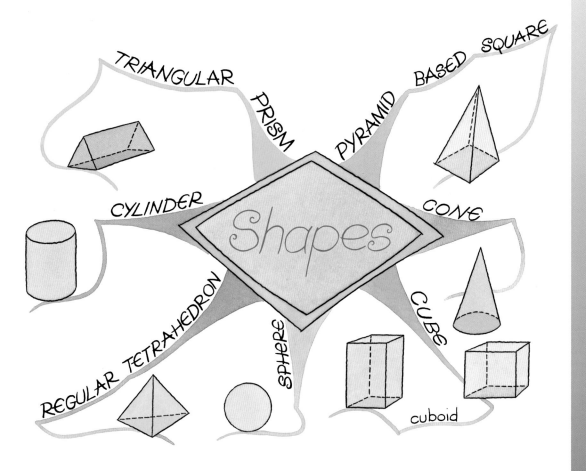

Shapes Mind Map

Collecting Data

Do you ever need to **collect** information or do surveys for Maths projects? Might you then have to remember your **working** methods and the **results** in exams? Mind Maps are useful tools for instant reading of survey results. All the collected data is present on one sheet of paper and it's easy to understand. For example, supposing you and your friends were asked to **count** different types of vehicles for a traffic **survey** for a morning. You would have to find a way of representing your findings. You could use a symbol to represent, say, 10 cars and then put this on your Mind Map. It would then be very easy to **calculate how many** cars you had seen in total. You could then **subdivide** them into different **colours** of cars.

Don't forget to include a 'key' on your Mind Map, so that everyone knows what the various **symbols** mean.

The example on the next page shows how many vehicles and pedestrians were using a busy junction during a one-hour period in September. The researchers made a **record** of their counting on a note pad and then **drew** the Mind Map properly later on.

September Rush Hour Survey

Cars

Red 22   Blue 41   Green 30   White 28   Other 36

卌 卌 卌 卌   卌 卌 卌 卌   卌 卌 卌 卌 卌   卌 卌 卌 卌 卌   卌 卌 卌 卌 卌
|| 卌 卌 卌 卌 | | 卌 ||| 卌 卌 卌 |

Taxis

Black cabs 33   Others 21

卌 卌 卌 卌 卌   卌 卌 卌 卌 |
卌 卌 卌 |||

Buses

Double-deckers 30   Single 12   Coaches 14

卌 卌 卌 卌 卌   卌 卌 || 卌 卌 ||||
卌 卌

Cycles

Cyclists with helmets 12   Cyclists without 31

卌 卌 || 卌 卌 卌 卌 卌
            卌 卌 |

Pedestrians

Men 48   Women 57   Children walking 23   Children in buggies 20

卌 卌 卌 卌 卌   卌 卌 卌 卌 卌   卌 卌 卌 卌 卌   卌 卌 卌 卌
卌 卌 卌 卌 卌   卌 卌 卌 卌 卌 ||| 卌 卌 卌 卌
卌 ||| 卌 卌 卌 卌 ||

September Rush Hour Survey Mind Map

=10
=10
=10
+6
Total = 36

other

red

+2
Total = 22

CARS

blue

green

+1
Total = 41

white

Total = 30

+8
Total = 28

TAXIS

other

+1

buggies

black

+3

alking

+3

To decode Mind Map data:
each picture = 10 sightings
each flag = single sightings

Mind Mapping Science

Mind Maps for **Science** can be used to remember **processes** and to organize information when you are **revising**.

Life Cycles

One of the **important** things you will need to learn is the **Cycles of Life**. Everything that is alive on this planet goes through a cycle of change as it grows and develops, but some are a little different from others and it is important to **remember** the **differences**. For example: a chicken's egg, with its hard, protective shell, is laid by the hen, who then keeps it warm until the fluffy chick hatches out. This then grows into a pullet – a young chicken  – which finally develops into a fully grown chicken. **Contrast** this with the human baby, who is born completely helpless, growing gradually into a child, a teenager and then into an independent adult.

You could **compare** different types of life cycle by putting them on **one** Mind Map. This would help you **revise** more easily and Mind Maps are a lot more **fun** than boring lists. The Mind Map on page 69 is one example of how you could sum up this information with a Mind Map.

Whats the longest piece of furniture in the school?

The multiplication table.

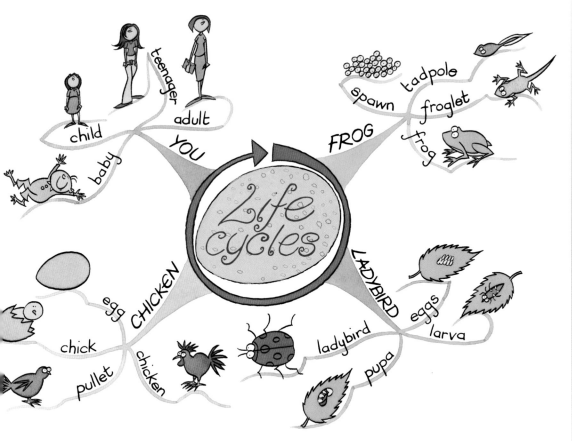

Life Cycles Mind Map

Reversible and Irreversible Changes

You will also need to know all about **reversible** and **irreversible** changes. A Mind Map will help you revise the information and remember it better in exams. No need for any confusion now! Your brain will remember where on your Mind Map you have drawn your **pictures** and this will **remind** you what the information is.

You can choose whatever **examples** of changes you like. Use your Mind Map to help you work out whether the process is reversible or irreversible. What does reversible mean? Well, it means that if you cause something to change, you can then change it back to what it was in the first place. For example, take butter (yeah, but not in your hot hand!). It is cold when it comes out of the fridge, but when you have left it lying in the hot kitchen it will start to melt. Later, you can return it to the fridge and it will harden again. It will become the same as it was before. It has gone through a **reversible change**!

What does irreversible change mean? Still in the kitchen (where lots of irreversible changes happen every day!), you might want to cook an egg. Well, the egg is runny inside when you take it out of the fridge. But after five minutes in boiling water or the frying pan, the yolk and white become firmer and less runny. If you leave the egg in the pan for 10 minutes both yolk and white will go completely hard – gruesome if it's a fried egg, but perfect if you want a hard-boiled egg! (Just the snack to have when you feel you need a little break from revision!) And you can't change it back to what it was in the first place. It's gone through an irreversible change.

Have a look at these **changes** and make a **Mind Map** which **sorts** them out. Add as many **details** about the process as you can, just by **extending** the little branches.

Changes

Freezing

Dissolving

Evaporating

Melting

Burning

Cooking

Think up your own **examples** to illustrate the two kinds of changes. For example, if you love eating chocolate (which a lot of people seem to!) you could use it as an example for melting – couldn't you? You'd be bound to **remember** drawing a bar of chocolate on your Mind Map and that would **remind** you that it is an example of a reversible change! Compare your Mind Map with then one on pages 72–3.

Tony's Mind Map Tips for Science

Mind Maps will help you:

★ *Remember processes*
★ *Organize information*
★ *Remember scientific facts and data*

hardens
heat
melts

hardens
heat
melts

chocolate
butter
ice-lolly
hardens
heat
melts

REVERSIBLE

melting

freezing

evaporation

ice-cube

water

melts

sun

refrozen

vap

72 **Reversible and Irreversible Changes Mind Map**

ash

wood

burning

IRREVERSIBLE

cooking

nges

dissolving

eggs

fried

hard boiled

coffee

granules liquid

cooks

condenses

droplets

Mind Mapping History

You already tried out a **Mind Map** for History at the beginning of this book, when we looked at Mind Mapping the Fire of London (*see pages 20–1*). Let's take another look at how Mind Maps can **help** you with **History.** As we saw with the Fire of London, you can use Mind Maps to **summarize** information during your revision. Here's another example. Suppose you need to be able to **recall facts** about, or write an essay on, Elizabeth I and the Armada in your exam. The information you need to **revise** from is probably in an uninspiring block of text in your History textbook, a bit like the extract below.

Elizabeth I and the Armada

The relationship between England and Spain during the reign of Elizabeth I (1558–1603) was not friendly. The Catholic King of Spain, Philip, wanted to remove Elizabeth and replace her with her Catholic cousin, Mary, Queen of Scots. Because she kept plotting to kill Elizabeth, everyone thought that Philip was behind the plots, so Elizabeth did not stop Francis Drake and others attacking Spanish ships and lands. Drake's three-year trip to Spanish colonies in South America, capturing ships and gold, enraged the Spanish and in 1588 Philip decided to invade England. A fleet of 130 ships and 30,000 men, called the Armada, set sail for England, the intention being to take on board a further 20,000 men in Spanish Netherlands. The plan was to destroy the English navy on the way, using an outdated method of running alongside and pulling two vessels together using grappling irons.

With superior cannons, up-to-date techniques and knowledge of local weather patterns, Drake played bowls as the Armada made its way past Plymouth. Drake's plan was to pick off the galleons one by one from behind. This he did, but his Secret Formula was to fill old vessels with kindling and gunpowder and set them to drift among the Spanish craft. Eventually the fleet was scattered and wrecked around the Scottish and Irish coastlines.

What a boring block of text! OK, read it through once more (one last time – after this you can just **refer** to your Mind Map!) and **pick** out what you think are the most **important** points – a highlighter pen might help. **Summarize** these in your own Mind Map and then see how well you can remember all the **information**. (Pretty well, I'd say.) **Compare** your Mind Map with the one on the next page – remember there is no one correct answer.

Tony's Mind Map Tips for History

Mind Maps will help you:

★ *Take **notes** from one source or several*
★ **Plan** *essays*
★ *Sort out and remember **facts***
★ **Sort** *out and remember the order of events*

Why does history keep repeating itself?

Because we weren't listening the first time!

Elizabeth I and the Armada Mind Map

Elizabeth

Protestant

gold

loot   attack   ships

South

America

DRAKE

England

old   technique   Spanish   attack

galleons

bowls   Scotland

wrecks   cannons

The Egyptians and Tutankhamun

Here is how you can use Mind Mapping to gather information from a variety of sources and take notes in a form that you can understand later on, when you are revising. This is useful if you 'read around' the subject and gather information from several different books, TV programmes or the internet.

Here are some notes, from different sources, about Tutankhamun. Can you make them into a Mind Map? Don't forget, there are many different possibilities – all Mind Maps are different because all brains are different!

Tutankhamun became king at the age of nine and was married straight away to Ankhesenpaten. His father died in 1336BC and was buried in a secret tomb.

Tutankhamun was born c.1342BC by the River Nile to Akhenaten and Kiya, who was Akhenaten's second wife.

They worshipped the Sun god, Aten.

Tutankhamun restored the old religion and built new temples.

Tutankhamun was crowned at the temple at Karnak.

He was commander-in-chief of Egypt's army

Akhenaten's first wife was called Queen Nefertiti, who helped plan their garden-city. She had six daughters, who were Tutankhamun's half-sisters.

Tutankhamun was taught to read and write by scribes. He learnt hieroglyphics. Papyrus was used for writing on.

The army was armed with bronze daggers and swords, axes and clubs. They had ox-skin shields.

He learnt the family history from Ay, a government official.

He died in 1323BC at the age of 17 or 18, probably from a chariot accident.

His body was mummified so that he could go to the afterlife, and buried with many marvellous possessions in three coffins, one inside the other. The innermost one was solid gold.

He lay undisturbed until 1923, when Howard Carter opened the burial chamber.

The possessions were for him to use during his journey to the afterlife.

17 years 1323 BC chariot

accident

DIED

gold 3 coffins mummified

possessions

married 9 yrs KING

Karnak crowned temples

chief army

shields daggers

axes clubs religion old

The Egyptians and Tutankhamun Mind Map

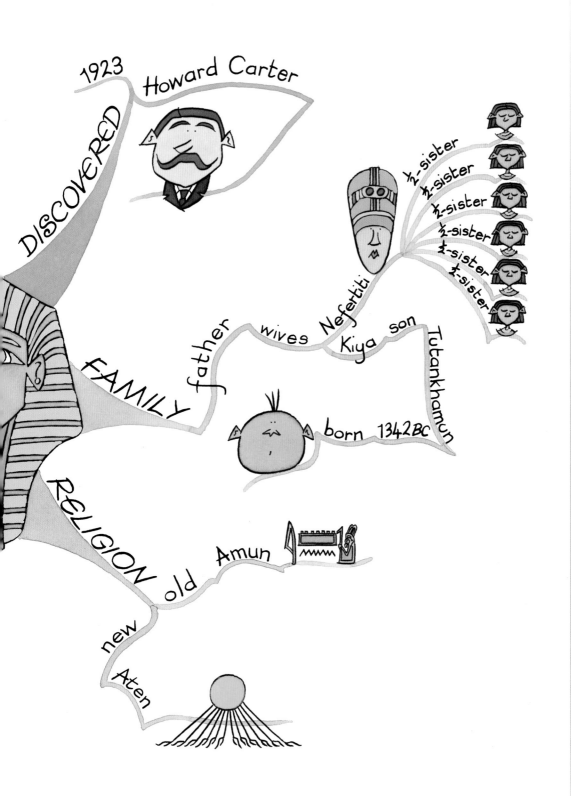

1923   Howard Carter

DISCOVERED

½-sister
½-sister
½-sister
½-sister
½-sister
½-sister

FAMILY   father   wives   Nefertiti   Kiya   son   Tutankhamun

born 1342BC

RELIGION   old   Amun

new   Aten

Mind Mapping Geography

Mind Maps are **excellent** tools for revising and remembering a **process** and will help you sort and **order** the information you need to learn.

Volcanoes

Take volcanoes for example. Can you **remember** all the various important aspects of vulcanization that you need to know? A Mind Map will **help** you out!

Here are the facts, as you might find them in a textbook or reference book. Have a quick **read** through, sort out what the **important** facts are and then see if you can **create** your own Mind Map. Compare yours with the version on the next page.

Volcanoes occur when a fissure or weakness in the Earth's crust allows molten rock, called magma, ashes and gases to escape. The magma is under great pressure and a weakness in the crust allows it to become lava and flow out. As it cools it solidifies. The volcano's cone is made up of layers of lava and ash from former eruptions. The wide opening at the top of the volcano is called the crater, surrounded by the rim. In recently erupted volcanoes the craters are full of pools of molten rock, bubbling with gases. In older volcanoes all that remains is solid rock, sometimes filled with a lake. Inside the volcano a pipe, or opening, leads down to the magma. Its top is called a vent, which is sometimes blocked by a plug of hardened lava. Right down at the bottom of the pipe is a pool of magma called a magma chamber. Some volcanoes erupted many years ago and are now dormant (or 'sleeping'), while others are still active and could erupt again at any time. There are between 20 and 30 active volcanoes in the world that erupt each year. An example is Nevado del Ruiz in Colombia, South America. Dormant volcanoes include Mount Fujiyama in Japan, which last erupted in 1707, and Mount Rainier in the United States, which has not erupted for over 100 years. A volcano is extinct when it has not erupted for thousands of years. Two examples are Mount Egremont in the USA and Mount Kilimanjaro in Tanzania.

Who's the
world's deadliest
baker?

Attila the
Bun!

Tony's Mind Map Tips for Geography

Mind Maps will help you:

- ★ **Understand** *geographic processes*
- ★ **Organize** *information*
- ★ **Summarize** *and remember facts*
- ★ **Remember** *which countries make up which continents, and the names of capital cities*

How did the
Vikings send secret
messages?

By Norse
code!

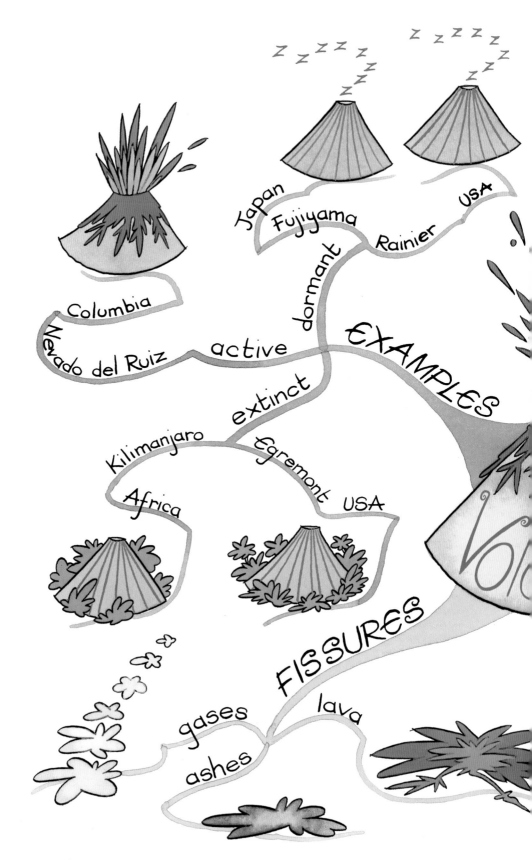

EXAMPLES

Japan
Fujiyama
USA
Rainier
dormant

Columbia
Nevado del Ruiz
active

extinct

Kilimanjaro
Egremont
USA
Africa

FISSURES

gases
ashes
lava

CROSS-SECTION

pipe

vent

magma

CRATER

rim

lake

noes

Mind Mapping Languages

Using a Mind Map is the **perfect** way to revise words in a foreign language. The **pictures** you draw remind your **brain** of the words.

Pick a Colour

For example, you can use the **colours** of your Mind Map *(see below)* to help you remember the names of the colours in French, and the **pictures** give your brain a little nudge if you forget.

Even better, you can **group** together vocabulary that you'll need to **learn** for different topics or role-playing scenarios. When it comes to exams, written or oral, you'll be able to **remember** all the words for a given topic thanks to your Mind Maps – **SORTED!**

Mind Map Shopping List

The Mind Map example on pages 88–9 shows French **words** you might need to **learn** for a shopping role play. Again, the **pictures** help you remember.

Tony's Mind Map Tips for Languages

Mind Maps will help you:

★ **Revise** *and remember vocabulary*
★ *Remember words and phrases to* **role play** *different scenarios*
★ **Organize** *and remember key phrases to use in essays*

le miel

le confiture

les céréales

les boissons

les pâtes

ÉPICER...

le gâteau

les biscuits

BOULANGERIE

le pain

les oeufs

la crème

le lait

LAITERIE

le yaourt

le fromage

French Vocabulary for Shopping Role Play Mind Map

MARCHAND DE

FRUITS

les pommes

bananes les

oranges les

LÉGUMES

les tomates

la salade

carottes les

pommes de terre les

CHARCUTERIE

les saucisses

porc le

terrine la

S

es

Mind Mapping Citizenship

Citizenship is about **developing** your knowledge and **understanding** about becoming an **informed** and **responsible** person when it comes to things like looking after the Earth and its finite **resources** or understanding how legal systems work. **Recycling** is one area you may be asked about.

Reuse it, Don't Lose it!

Responsible use of the Earth's **resources** is all-important. We consume a lot, so we should reuse a lot too! We all use a lot of glass on a daily basis. What happens to those bottles and jars once you've used up the **contents**? Does it get thrown into the dustbin or do you live in an area where there is a recycling collection? Glass is not **biodegradable**. That means that it does not rot

and it never will. However, it can be remelted and remoulded many times over, without losing any of its **quality**. If you can recycle glass – do! **Separate** out the **different** colours if you are using a bottle bank. You taking trouble to do this means that it can be **reused** again and again.

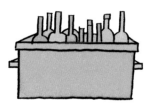

What Are all the Possible Options?

You buy the glass bottle in a shop, take it home and use the **contents**. What happens next? If you throw it into your dustbin it will be taken to a landfill site with all your other **rubbish** and refuse. But it will just stay there – forever – or it will be incinerated and the glass is useless. It cannot **biodegrade**. You may be lucky enough to be able to get money back if you return your bottles to the shop. This used to happen, but is less common these days. Bottles taken to a **bottle bank** or collected in kerbside collections are broken and the glass is taken off to be remoulded and made into more bottles, which may eventually make their way back to your **house** again!

How about Tins and Cans?

Do you drink fizzy drinks? What do you do with the **empty tins**? If you throw them away in the dustbin they are just dumped in the landfill site with all the other **rubbish**. However, if you recycle, either by using a kerbside collection or can bank, the metal can be **reprocessed** into new cans. Sackfuls are collected by charities and community groups as they can be resold. Aluminium has a higher scrap value than steel, so it is good if you can **separate** the cans out from each other (test with a magnet – if it sticks then the can is steel). At the processing plant, the can is **shredded**. The steel is compressed into bales and sold to the steel industry. Aluminium is sent for remelting and **manufactured** into new **products**.

See if you can put this information into a Mind Map for **easy revision**.

remoulded

reused

Kerbside

GLASS

landfill

dustbin

incinerator

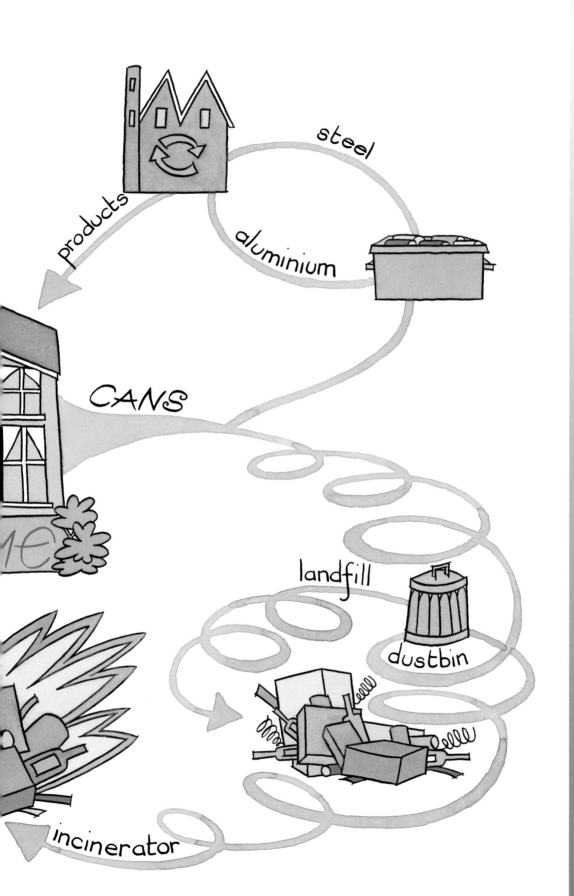

steel

aluminium

products

CANS

landfill

dustbin

incinerator

Tony's Mind Map Tips for Citizenship

Mind Maps will help you:

★ Sort out processes
★ Remember important facts
★ Understand connections between important causes and events

New refuse collector:
So will I get
any training?

Old timer:
No, you just
pick it up as you
go along.

Mind Maps for EVERYTHING!

So you see, Mind Maps can help you in all your **subjects** – and not just the ones shown here. Be **inventive** and make them work for you the way **YOU** want them to. That's what they're there for, to help you **SUCCEED**!

Your memory has an INFINITE capacity to remember if you use it well – and with Mind Maps you will!

Third Reminder

'Five-times repetition equals long-term memory'

Tony's Mind Map Tips

Reminder: What are Mind Maps for?

Mind Maps help you ...

REMEMBER

SORT OUT *information and ideas*

CONCENTRATE

be CREATIVE

use your IMAGINATION

UNDERSTAND

TAKE NOTES

STAY COOL

TAKE CONTROL

STAY INTERESTED

Don't Let it Get to You!

Stressed-out with revision? Try out some calming techniques to keep you really cool!

Do you ever hear people saying, 'I feel SO stressed-out'? Well, we all get a bit stressed-out from time to time. It's normal! In fact, we probably couldn't manage without a little bit of healthy stress to get us up and **running** and keep us on our toes. If we stayed **calm** and **cool** all the time, maybe we'd never get motivated to do ANYTHING at all! We'd just stay in bed loafing, saying, 'Don't worry, I'll be fine when the exams come round. I don't need to do any **revision**.' (Just imagine how your mum and dad would react to that!) So, a little bit of stress gets us **moving** and **motivates** us to **DO** something.

But **too** much stress is a bad thing and can make us depressed and ill. It can make us panic and feel out of control, so that we feel unable to do anything at all. If you feel a bit like this, try some of the **suggestions** in this chapter for de-stressing. They really do work and are **simple** and **easy** to do.

Don't Bottle it Up

However, if you really do feel under a lot of stress, so much that you feel you can't carry on **normally**, and that everything is getting on top of you, the best thing to do is to try to **share** your thoughts with someone else – your parents, a mate, anybody you feel **comfortable** talking to.

Remember, you are very much brainier than you think. It's just a matter of mining for the nuggets of information in your brain when you are revising and taking exams. Mind Maps help you strike gold!

Coping with normal stress and staying **chilled** will help you to **succeed** in your revising and when you are taking the actual exams. This is really one of the major keys to the door labelled SUCCESS. When you are relaxed you will be able to **concentrate**, **remember** things, **plan** and **organize** – in fact, everything you need for exams.

Doodle Down-time

Have you noticed something about **Mind Maps** yet? If you have done a few already you'll know that the very act of making a Mind Map **calms** you down. Just getting going with your **felt-tip pens** and letting your mind **daydream** from one idea to another, and the doodling that you do when you draw the little **pictures**, all help to **chill** you out.

De-stressing Techniques for Mental Athletes

Try these **calming** techniques. Olympic athletes use them to help them get ready for their big races, which is very much like taking an exam.

1. Give Your Brain a Break

This technique will relax your mind and calm those butterflies in your tummy.

- ★ *Sit at your desk with your hands loosely in your lap and your feet flat on the floor.*
- ★ *Close your eyes.*
- ★ *Think of a small pond. It could be one that you know, or you can imagine one.*
- ★ *Think of yourself standing by the pond.*
- ★ *Sniff the air. What can you smell? Newly mown grass? Scented flowers?*

- ★ *Pick up a smooth pebble from the ground at your feet. Notice its smoothness against your skin.*
- ★ *Throw it gently into the water.*
- ★ *Hear the little splash it makes.*
- ★ *See the water splash upwards.*
- ★ *Watch the water close over the pebble as it sinks.*
- ★ *Watch the rings of ripples spreading out and vanishing.*
- ★ *Watch the water become smooth again.*
- ★ *Watch the butterflies fluttering across the smooth water.*

2. Take a Long Deep Breath

This technique is useful for all sorts of stressful situations and is a good one to use before you start revising or when you first sit down at your desk in an exam.

★ *Sit at your desk with your hands loose in your lap and your feet flat on the floor.*

★ *Close your eyes.*

★ *Start breathing in deeply, without making any breathing noises. Think about your breath going in and nothing else.*

★ *Hold briefly.*

★ *Then breathe out, deeply. Think about your breath going out and nothing else.*

★ *Repeat about 10 times, breathing more deeply with each breath.*

★ *You should now be feeling wonderfully calm and relaxed – ready for anything!*

3. Laugh it Off!

Make sure you have a good laugh every day. Laughter is one of the best ways to relax and makes you feel **positive** about **everything**.

What do ghosts do at 11am?

Take a coffin break!

4. If You Snooze, You Won't Lose

Do you find it **difficult** to get to **sleep**, or do you wake up in the early hours worrying about exams or all the revision that needs doing? You could try having a hot bedtime drink. **Avoid** drinking fizzy drinks, tea or coffee in the evenings. They all contain brain-zapping caffeine, which can keep you awake. It may sound a bit hippyish but **aromatherapy** can really help you chill. (Those hippies are masters at chilling.) Try sprinkling a few drops of lavender essence on your pillow or in your bath. The lavender helps calm and soothe you.

Alternatively, try this amazingly calming exercise to help get you off to sleep. Again, this is what the best athletes do before important competitions.

★ *Lie on your back in bed, with your arms loosely at your sides.*

★ *Close your eyes and think about each part of your body in turn.*

★ *Start off by thinking about your feet. Tighten them for a few moments, hold, and then relax them completely.*

★ *Think about your calves. Tighten for a few moments, hold, then relax.*

★ *Think about your thighs. Tighten for a few moments, hold, then relax.*

★ *Think about your abdomen. Tighten for a few moments, hold, then relax.*

★ *Think about your shoulders. Tighten for a few moments, hold, then relax.*

★ *Think about your back. Tighten for a few moments, hold, then relax.*

★ *Think about your face. Scrunch it up as much as you can, hold, then relax.*

★ *Lastly, think about all 10 fingers. Clench them as much as you can, hold, then relax.*

If you are still awake after this, try the pond visualization exercise again *(see page 100)*.

You can also do this during the **day**, when you need to relax for half an hour. Try doing it while you are **playing** some relaxing **music**. It doesn't matter if you have a little **doze**. In fact, it's a brilliant idea. You'll wake up after a while and feel fully **refreshed**.

5. Don't Go it Alone – Start a Revision Club

You may feel a bit lonely sitting in your room revising all the time. What are all your mates up to? Are they really revising, or are they just saying they are? Does it seem as though the rest of your life is on hold during the exam season?

Well, here's a solution. Why not get together with your friends on a regular basis to revise with MIND MAPS! All you need to do is arrange a regular time, where to meet (e.g. someone's house) and which subject to tackle. Maybe you could try them all in rotation, one on each day.

When you've chosen the topic you want to discuss, get all your books together and have a **good brainstorm** – different people have different views about the same thing, so you'll come up with **lots more ideas** than you would on your own. Of course, the best way to brainstorm something is with a Mind Map. You can each do one on your chosen subject and then discuss your different versions.

> *Talking around a subject helps bring it to life and will help give you new ideas, as well as fix the old ideas in your head. Two (or three, or four) brains are better than one!*

Alternatively, you could do one **big group Mind Map** (tape together a few sheets of plain A3 paper) and discuss what you think the main branches should be and then brainstorm the sub-branches. You will be **amazed** at the number of ideas you come up with!

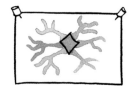

Another idea would be to take it in turns to **build up** the Mind Map as you pass it around from person to person – when it's your go you add an extra branch or sub-branch.

Getting together in this way means you get to see your **mates**, have a **laugh** AND **revise** – don't think that revision is all about social exile!

Fourth Reminder

'Five-times repetition equals long-term memory'

Who designed Noah's ark?

An ark-itect!

Tony's Top De-stressing Tips

★ Have a **laugh** (or laughs) every day.

★ Take some good-quality **exercise** every day (and this doesn't mean walking from your bedroom to the kitchen and back again!).

★ Try out some simple **meditation** (it's not whacky!).

★ Try out some simple **visualization** (this is simply using your imagination).

★ Have **music** in your room as a de-stressing background to your revision.

Exam Attack

On your marks, get set, GO!

Your revision time is up.

Now's the time to EXCEL!

On the evening before the exam, try to do something else apart from revision. Go **swimming**, talk to a friend and try to get a proper night's sleep. In the morning, eat a **good breakfast** that will see you through all morning. If you go into an exam feeling hungry, your brain will only want to think about **food**.

If you are allowed to wear non-uniform clothes, choose your most comfortable ones. **Check** your bag to make sure that you have everything you need with you: **pens**, spare ink cartridges, **pencils**, **felt-tip pens**, **a rubber**, **pencil sharpener**, a **ruler**, a **calculator** and any other mathematical instruments. You don't need a lucky **mascot** – you've got **Mind Maps!** If you are allowed to take a set book into the exam with you, check that you have it. Also take some **tissues** and a **watch**. Remember to take a loo break before you go into the exam room.

Chic Technique

Exams are not just about being able to **remember** stuff on the day, but also a lot about exam **TECHNIQUE**.

Part of this is knowing the kind of **questions** that you'll be asked on the day, and your **teachers** are definitely the best people to ask about this. Quite often they will have **practice** papers that you can look at to familiarize yourself with the style and format. This means that when you turn over your exam paper on the day it'll seem like you've done it before and you'll **immediately** feel more confident – especially as you've been doing all that effective revision. If you feel **confident** you'll be well on the way to getting those grades you know you deserve. It's going to be a breeze!

> *Ignore any of your friends who are fiendishly writing away right from the start.*

Exam technique is also about **tackling** your exam paper in the right way. You've got **ALL** the facts and information in that **amazing** brain of yours and they're not going to evaporate the moment you start reading the questions. So don't immediately regurgitate **EVERYTHING** you know about the subject. The chances are you're only being asked about one area in that subject. So take a moment before you start **writing**. Think of these five simple steps before you get going:

1. READ BEFORE YOU WRITE

★ *Deep breathing. Do a short deep-breathing exercise when you first sit down in the exam room (see page 101). Four or five deep breaths will calm any nerves.*

★ *Read right through.* When you first turn over the paper, take a few minutes to read right through the whole paper very carefully and make sure that you have grasped all the instructions. Reading all the questions ahead of answering them gives your brain the chance to subconsciously work on later questions while you are at work on the earlier ones.

★ **Easy comes first.** If there are choices to be made – choose the easiest ones to do first.

★ *Time it right.* Work out how much time you should spend on each question and stick to it. The way you manage your time in exams is half the battle.

★ **Reap your rewards.** In the exam, look for the questions that are worth the most marks and spend more time on these than ones worth fewer marks. This is called 'harvesting' points.

Why did the child study in the aeroplane?

Because he wanted a higher education.

Fifth Reminder

'Five-times repetition equals long-term memory'

2. MASTER IT WITH MIND MAPS

★ *Plan before pen.* Spend a minute or two quickly Mind Mapping the answer to each question, so that you can remember the relevant things quickly and have them written down in front of you.

★ *Max the facts.* Remember, put the main point in the centre and your sub-topics on the main branches. All less-important topics are on the tiniest branches. Using the same colours that you used when you were revising will help your brain remember the facts you now need. Any pictures you draw should only be quick sketches.

★ *Essays for excellence.* If you are writing an essay-style answer, remember to plan an introduction, a middle and a conclusion.

★ *Share them, impress them.* Hand in your Mind Maps with your exam papers, not forgetting to put your name on them. They may count as 'extra working'.

3. WRITE IT RIGHT

★ *Rough before you write.* Think of the Mind Maps you do as your 'rough' answer to a question. When you do a Mind Map first, it is so much easier to write your final, complete 'neat' version.

★ *Neat's a feat.* Write up your neat version, checking things like spellings and punctuation.

Exam Attack

If you ever get stuck, think of the music you often play in your room at home – this may help bring back the information you need.

4. READ TO LEAD

★ *Check for changes.* Read through your answer. If you discover a mistake, cross it out neatly and write your correction over it.

★ *Your name's the game.* Remember to put your name on everything you hand in.

5. REST AND BE READY

★ *Rest for the best.* When you have finished a question take a deep breath and immediately read the next question. Then spend a minute or two with your eyes closed, doing some deep breathing. Whilst you are relaxing your brain will subconsciously be working on the next answer. You'll find your ideas flow much better when you continue.

Ignore people who keep going off to get more paper to write on. Remember it's quality, not quantity, that matters in the end. That said, because your brain will be fired up with Mind Maps, it will probably be you who is writing more – quality AND quantity!

What runs but never walks?

Water.

What a Breeze!

Well done! You made it! And we hope that Mind Mapping helped you through to SUCCESS.

Why not throw a special party? But what do you need to plan your party? Yes, you've got it! A Mind Map!

Tropical Party Mind Map

WHO?

friends

Abbie

Joel

Joss

Zoë

Sam

THEME

tropical

garlands

skirts

grass

sarongs

shirts

Hawaian

GAMES

dancing

limbo

coconut-shy

fancy-dress

competition

What a Breeze!

Resources

Make the most of your mind today!

You can now make fantastic Mind Maps on your computer thanks to a brilliant new interactive Mind Map programme called iMindMap™. For your free 30-day trial of iMindMap visit **www.BuzanMindMap.com** and follow the instructions online.

THE BUZAN ORGANISATION

If you would like to get in touch with Tony Buzan or find out more about events and courses, please contact the Buzan Organisation or visit www.buzanworld.com

The Buzan Organisation
Harleyford Manor Estate
Henley Road
Marlow
Buckinghamshire SL7 2DX
United Kingdom

Tel: 0845 003 8949 (UK)
Tel: +44 845 003 8949 (International)

Index

aromatherapy 102

boredom 6, 15, 56, 68, 75
brain structure 8–9, 15, 32, 52
breakfast 108
breaks 44–5
breathing exercise 101, 109, 112

checkmap 29
citizenship 90–4
clubs 103–4
colour 8–11, 15, 24, 27–8
    data collection 64
    picking 86
    revising 32, 42, 111
    shapes 62
    stories 56
    thinking 52
computers 37
confidence 48–9, 109

data collection 64–5
daydreaming 4, 8, 32–3, 99
de-stressing techniques 100–5
distractions 37
doodling 32, 99

Egypt map 80–1
empty house map 58–9
English 56–61
essay writing 29–30, 33, 57–61, 74–5, 111
exam techniques 108–13
example maps
    changes 72–3
    Egypt 80–1
    empty house 58–9
    Fire of London 20–1
    friends 12–13
    hobby 30–1
    life cycles 69
    recycling 92–3
    revision 40–1
    rush-hour survey 66–7
    science topics 54–5

shapes 63
Spanish Armada 76–7
tropical party 116–17
volcanoes 84–5
exercise 45, 105
extra working 111

Fire of London map 20–1
five-time repetition
formula 7, 33, 38–9, 42, 46, 48, 94
French 86–9
friends map 12–13

geography 82–5

harvesting points 110, 111
history 74–81
hobby map 30–1
homework 38, 49

irreversible changes 69–73

keys 64

languages 86–9
laughter 102, 104–5
left side of brain 8–9, 15, 52
life cycles 68–9
loo breaks 108

maths 62–7
meditation 105
memory 7, 24–5, 32, 42–3, 46, 52, 62
mind maps
    checkmap 29
    citizenship 92–3
    clubs 103–4
    definition 11
    drawing instructions 26–7
    English 58–9
    exam techniques 111
    examples 12–13, 18–21, 30–1, 116–17
    French 88–9
    geography 84–5

history 76–7, 80–1
maths 63, 66–7
revision 40–1
role 52–3
science 54–5, 69, 72–3
shopping list 87
tips 25, 28, 36, 42, 62, 71, 75, 83, 87, 95
motivation 38, 98
music 103, 105, 112

notes 6, 25, 28, 37
    reading around 43
    revising 53
    sources 75
    understanding 78

organization 33, 36–7, 71, 83, 87, 99
overview 39–42, 53

panic 38, 44, 98
party map 116–17
pictures 9–11, 15, 24, 28
    changes 69
    overview 42
    remembering 87
    stress 99
    thinking 52
planning 24, 33, 38, 44
    essays 53, 57
    exams 111
    stress 99

questions 6, 29

reading
    the answers 112
    around 43, 47, 78
    the questions 109–10
recycling 90–3
relaxation exercises 100–1, 103
reversible changes 69–73
revision map 40–1
right side of brain 8–11, 15, 32, 52
rush-hour survey map 66–7

science 68–73
shapes 62–3
sleeping 102–3
Spanish Armada map 76–7
strengths 46–7
stress 38, 97–105
summaries 57, 74, 75, 83
surveys 64–7
symbols 64

television 37, 43, 44, 78
temptations 37
timing 110
tips 25, 28, 36, 95
    geography 83
    history 75
    languages 87
    maths 62
    revision 42
    science 71
tissues 108
treats 37, 46
tropical party map 116–17
Tutankhamun map 80–1

visualization exercise 100, 103, 105
volcanoes map 82–5

watches 108
weaknesses 46–7
website address 120